S0-DQR-808

BUY THIS BOOK ONLINE
www.wolverinepublishing.com/horse

DATE DUE

This book is no ⸺ our ability to
handle any circ ⸺ employ the
services of a pr ⸺ ublisher and
author assume ⸺ this book.

THE AUTHORS ⸺ RRANTIES,
EXPRESSED O ⸺)F THIS
BOOK, AND E> ⸺ NTY RE-
GARDING THE ⸺ IED HEREIN.
THE USER AS‹ ⸺ OOK.

Wolverine
PUBLISHING

HORSE TRA
By Fiona Lloyd.
Published and d

© 2005 Fiona Llo
All rights reserve ⸺ ıy form without
written permissic

Cover photo: F ⸺ Dave Pegg.
All maps courtes

ISBN# 0-972160

DEMCO, INC. 38-2931

Wolverine Publishing is continually expanding its range of guidebooks. If you have a manuscript or idea for a book, or would like to find out more about our company and publications, contact:
Dave Pegg
Wolverine Publishing
5439 County Rd 243
New Castle
CO 81647
970-984-2815
dave@wolverinepublishing.com
www.wolverinepublishing.com

Printed in China.

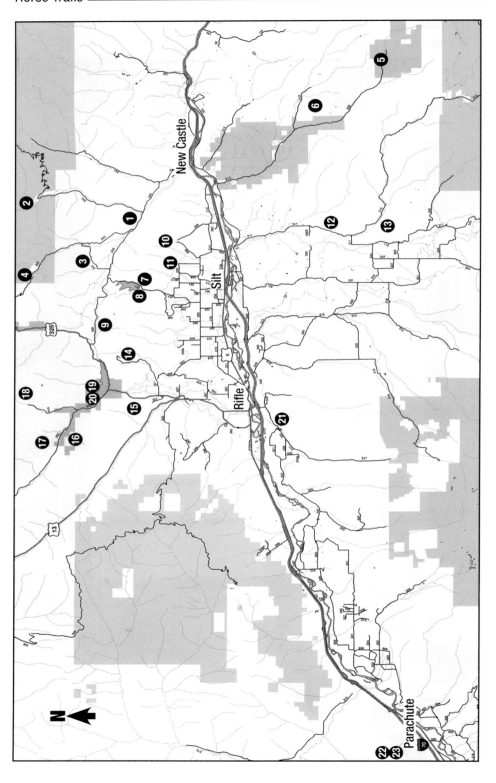

Contents

Introduction

I live within the boundaries of the White River National Forest. I have a choice of 5 trails to ride right outside my door. However, for the most part, these trails are of the "ride steeply uphill until you want to turn around and come back steeply downhill" variety. The White River National Forest is positively bristling with trails and if you want to trailer, camp and ride for a day or a couple of days, or especially beat the summer heat, that's the place to go. However, I mostly just want an easy, laid-back trail that I can ride while either conditioning my horses, or on a young horse—nothing too epic. Thus this book describes trails that are, for the most part, on BLM lands and not National Forest and are chosen with the following criteria in mind:

✦ Trails that I can trailer to within 1 hour and ride out and back within 2-6 hours —that way I can leave and get back in time to do chores.

✦ Where I can park and turn a 4 horse trailer with ease—unlike my neighbor, Chuck, I can't turn a trailer around on a dime!

✦ Where I can ride in quiet, beautiful countryside and where there are no potentially leg breaking sections of trail to negotiate (for the horse or rider!)

I have made notes on each trail—what you can expect to see, what you might encounter (both interesting and spooky), how steep the trail is etc. There is also a section for you to fill in when, and with whom, you did the trail with space for your own notes. I cannot recommend highly enough the addition to your day pack of flora and fauna guides—they expand the experience immensely. I also suggest a 'best season' to ride—just remember that in hunting season, even if you and your horse are painted bright orange, you risk being shot.

Date Ridden: *May 27th—my birthday!*

Partner: *Shadow Skipper*

Notes: *Met Jill and Brian at the old Columbine market. Saw a moose grazing! Lots of wildflowers in bloom—Indian paintbrush and Madonna lily*

There are many trails that I have left out. Access is a difficult subject and, although there may not be any physical signs of private ownership, I have, to the best of my ability, avoided any trails that cross private land. I have also tried to indicate private land close to trails on the maps. I did this by buying all the relevant USGS maps, BLM and White Forest maps and overlaying them with the public/private boundaries — this was necessarily a little inaccurate because of the differences in map scales! Please be respectful and read the access section that follows.

Please also consider getting involved by joining the Roaring Fork Valley Horse Council (www.roaringforkvalleyhorsecouncil.com, see advert page 24). It presents a unified voice, not only helping to preserve access to trails but also supporting the future welfare of horses and horsemanship. As the organisation grows, its aim is to eventually be a united voice for horsepeople from Aspen to Rifle and to inspire and assist other bordering areas to form horse councils.

The trail information tells you what map you need and gives you a rough idea of the time it will take to ride. The times don't account for stops and are timed at a fairly brisk walking pace. **Each trail is given a grade on a scale of 1-3 based on your horse's fitness.** Grade 1 is for horses that are just beginning to be ridden for the season. Grade 3 is for horses that are being ridden regularly two or three times a week.

In writing this book, I have assumed that each user will have all the necessary items for a comfortable ride (see trail etiquette) and either have reasonable riding skills or are with someone who does. Everything you do is at your own, and your horse's, risk. Finally, two points to bear in mind at all times: Potential Fire Hazards and Leave No Trace.

Access

Legal access to federal land is provided by a system of public and agency roads and trails. Public roads are intended to meet the transportation needs of the public user. Generally, a public road is any federal or state highway or county road administered by the state or county. BLM and USFS roads and trails are maintained for the administration and use of federal lands. Although generally open to the public, agency officials may restrict or control the use of these roads. Restrictions may be imposed for protection of sensitive or critical resources or to meet specific management needs. Land management agencies do not always have legal rights-of-way on all access roads or trails entering federal lands.

Private Lands

Two-thirds of the land area of the State of Colorado is privately owned. It is unlawful to enter private lands in Colorado without permission of the landowner. Colorado law does not require private lands to be marked, fenced or posted in any manner. Depending on the circumstances, trespass in Colorado may be prosecuted as a misdemeanor or as a felony. Additionally, the Colorado Revised Statutes state that "it is unlawful for any person to enter upon privately owned land or lands under the control of the State Board of Land Commissioners to take any wildlife by hunting, trapping, or fishing without first obtaining permission from the owner or person in possession of such land." The responsibility of knowing whether you are on private or public land is YOURS.

On non-navigable rivers and streams, the adjacent landowner's jurisdiction extends to the middle of the stream or river. Colorado law does allow floating access on a stream or river as long as no contact is made with the river bottom or shoreline while passing through (over) private lands.

How do I gain access to private lands?

"ASK FIRST" to get access to private lands and please respect the property of others. Responsible visitors or users always respect the land, whether it is private or public, and take care to leave it the way they found it. The landowner has the right to deny access on or across private lands and may charge an access or user fee for the use of those private lands.

Signs

Colorado law states that "no person may post, sign or indicate in any way that public lands within Colorado, not held under exclusive control or lease, are privately owned lands." It is unlawful to close a legal public access route or sign federal public lands with the intention of restricting public use. The BLM, USFS or Colorado Division of Wildlife (CDOW) should be advised about access problems and the illegal posting of signs on federal lands. Unless these situations are brought to the attention of agency officials, the problem cannot be corrected.

How do I recognize public access routes?

Major access routes or points of access to public lands are usually identified by signs with an agency logo. Most USFS roads and many BLM roads are marked with signs bearing road numbers and white arrows depicting routes open to motorized travel, or with signs giving mileage to a geographical location or recreation area. Access routes without signs will require that you have a detailed map showing landownership and roads/trails to identify legal access points.

Other trails

Garfield County extends all the way to the Utah border—a trail guide to all of Garfield County would be a massive tome! There are lots more trails out there—here are some ideas.

The White River National Forest bristles with trails. *The White River National Forest Map* shows all the trailheads—there are LOTS!

Cameo Wild Horse Management Area—a free pamphlet is available from the Grand Junction BLM office—great trail riding in winter and spring. A map of the BLM resource management areas is also free—invaluable for the section of Garfield not covered in this book and for trails surrounding Grand Junction—order from their website.

JQS Road, Rifle—I didn't include the numerous trails in this area because they are heavily used by others—often resulting in a very *un*-zen experience—but a detailed map, called *Mountain Biking the Roan Cliffs,* is available from Rifle Parks and Recreation at City Hall in Rifle. While you are in there, also pick up: *The Flattops Trail System and Trails in the West Flat Tops Plateau* for good National Forest Trails.

Other maps to have on hand are: *National Geographic Trails Illustrated—Rifle Gap, The White River National Forest Map,* and the BLM surface management status maps for Glenwood Springs and Carbondale. The BLM office in Glenwood Springs also has free maps to lots of other areas, including a pocket guide for Red Hill, The Roan Plateau (a travel map and visitor guide) and a trail map for Glenwood Springs.

If you see a potential trail on the map, remember that no time spent in reconnaissance is wasted—but always check out the parking and access before you trailer! Also, please don't hesitate to contact me, **fiona@wolverinepublishing.com**, if you think more information is needed on any of these trails, or if the trail changes significantly from what is published. Further, if you like this book, let me know and I'll write a National Forest Trail Guide!

Trail Etiquette

Be prepared. Let someone know where you are going and include your anticipated return time, then stick to your plan. This is critical if you are riding alone. Bring a good map and compass/GPS. Know the weather forecast. Be familiar with the signs of heat stress, dehydration, and hypothermia in people and horses, as well as treatment and prevention options. Always carry a first aid kit (human and horse), sunglasses, sunscreen, water, waterproofs, DEET, toilet paper, survival kit, bandana or hat, watch, whistle, knife, poncho and flashlight (with extra batteries). Other useful items include a spare 'shoe/boot', duct tape, nylon cord, leather strings, pliers and hoof pick. Bring plenty of food. Cell phones will be useless in many remote areas; however, you may get reception on top of a mountain in an emergency. Trail ride within the ability of your physical fitness and the condition of your horse. Train before trail riding. Get your horse used to other horses, cattle, hikers, backpackers, mountain bikes, vehicles (including off-road), and anything else they could encounter on a multi-user trail. Consider wearing a helmet; basic white is recommended; you will be seen more easily by others. Check your tack and the condition of your horse's shoes before you start out. Keep an eye on the condition of your horse and travel at a pace that is safe for the terrain or weather conditions.

Be a good representative. You represent all trail riders when on the trail and how you act influences people's opinions of all horseback riders. Respect and be courteous to all other users. Follow the rules of the area where you are riding. Leave gates as you find them. When you leave the trail (and parking area), leave only hoof prints.

Other users. Horseback riders have the right-of-way over all other users. Vehicles (including off-road) should yield to all other users. Bikers should yield to both horseback riders and hikers. Hikers should yield to horseback riders. Don't assume that everyone is familiar with these rules. If it appears that another user is not going to yield to you, politely ask them to stop (and thank them) while you pass. Pass everyone at a walk. Ride on the right and pass left shoulder to left shoulder. When approaching another user from the rear, call out "hello" as soon as you get close enough to make them aware of your presence. If going around someone, call out to them asking if it is OK to pass and tell them which side you want to pass. If someone wants to pass you, stop and/or pull over. Downhill users should yield to uphill users. Thank everyone for yielding as you pass.

Riding with others. Make sure all riders are ready and mounted before you ride off. Find out the experience level of unfamiliar riders before you start out. Know your group if you are leading. Always keep your group together and let the slowest person set the pace. Keep up with the rider in front of you. If necessary, separate the group into smaller groups of slow and fast riders. Keep your horse under control at all times. Don't pick up the pace or take off unannounced; it is not only rude but can be dangerous. Don't crowd other horses. Tell everyone if you are riding a green horse or if your horse kicks (i.e. tie a red ribbon in the tail). Stop before any crossing to make sure all the horses in a group cross together, and cross at a walk. When stopping to water your horse and/or the horses in your group, make sure all the horses have finished drinking before you move on.

Water. Bring and drink plenty of water during the warmer months. The availability of water on the trails varies seasonally, so have some waiting at the trailer for your horse when you return. Encourage your horse to drink as often and as much as it wants.

Tying your horse. Never tie using the reins and always use a quick-release knot. Using trail bridles, which have built-in halters, is recommended. If you don't use trail bridles, bring a halter and lead rope.

Hunting. Be familiar with the different hunting seasons. If you are on the trail during hunting season, wear blaze orange vests and make lots of noise (talking, singing, bells). Staying off the trails during big-game gun season is recommended.

Lightning. Lightning can travel far ahead of a storm. If you see or hear a thunderstorm aproaching, seek shelter immediately and wait for the storm to pass. Make sure you do not get caught in the water, on an exposed ridge, under large, solitary trees, or in the open. Seek shelter in low-lying areas, such as dense stands of small trees. Stay away from anything that attracts lightning. Get off your horse, get in a crouch position, and place both feet on the ground. Everyone should stay about 50 feet apart.

Getting lost. Don't panic if you get lost. Take a break and relax for a few minutes. Check your map and take a reading with your compass/GPS. If you can, backtrack to the last point where you knew you were still on the trail. If you can't find familiar ground, stop and stay where you are. Since someone is expecting your return, when you don't, they will send help.

Fences and Cattle. If you have to cross a range fence, please replace the gate as you found it. Make sure your dogs are obedient around cattle.

Dogs. Generally speaking, all the trails are OK for dogs. Where they aren't (eg Garfield Creek Wildlife Area) I've noted it. Some trails require some road riding—make sure your dog is obedient or leashed around traffic.

Guns. I have been told to carry one for the following reasons:
  1) Riding alone.
  2) Lion or bear.
  3) To summon help (Three regular shots. Wait 1 minute, three more regular shots.) and to defend yourself whilst injured
  4) If the worst happens, and your horse breaks its leg

Winter riding. Dress for the occasion and be careful to cool and dry your horse off afterwards. Horse trailers can sink into the mud as it defrosts during the day— returning to a trailer up to its axles is no fun!

New Castle

	Grade
1. Teakee Mine Road	2
2. Deep Creek	3
3. West Elk Loop	2
4. Cherry Stock Trail	2
5. Baldy Creek	2
6. Center Mountain	2

New Castle

Silt

Rifle

Rulison

Parachute

Teakee Mine Road

Grade: 2
Type: Out and back
Time: 3-5 hours
USGS Quad: Deep Creek

Description: The trail follows an old mine road up to the crest of the ridge (3 hours there and back) to an overlook where you can either turn around or follow the crest northwest, dropping back to the northeast to end in a sagebrush mesa with views to the east. The Teakee Mine was a uranium mine and the yellow mineral in the tailings is carnotite. Don't take any home as a souvenir!

Notes & Directions: Exit I70 N to New Castle, turn L or west into town. Take 7th Street N out of New Castle which becomes CR245. Turn R or N on CR243—Main Elk. The trail is 0.5m on your left. There is limited parking here and a good turn around at mile marker 1. There is also ample parking and turning space at the intersection of CR245 and 243.

As the trail faces east, this can be a good trail to do early on hot mornings. The upper parts retain snow, but not too deeply, so it can also be a good winter ride.

There are also a number of good shorter conditioning loops you can do on the trails on the slopes below the mine. Note that there is a lot of 'junk' around the old cabin.

Date Ridden:

Partner:

Notes:

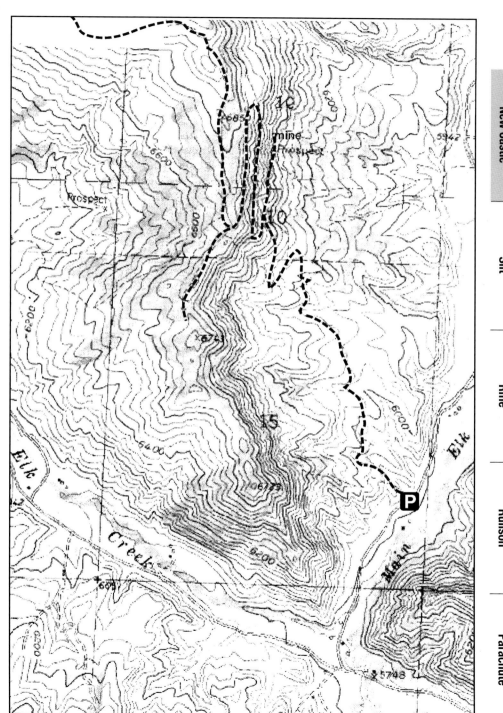

Deep Creek

Grade: 3
Type: Out and back
Time: 4 hours
USGS Quad: Deep Creek

I thought long and hard before including this trail. In the end, I decided that its 'pros' outweighed the 'cons', but this trail is not for novice riders and absolutely not for unseasoned trail horses.

The pros are: It is very beautiful. It is one of the very few trails best done in July, Aug and Sept. It is a great overnight stop, with trout fishing for dinner.

The cons are: Sections with potential for 'epics'. In describing these sections I would rather you felt that I had overstated than understated them.

The trail only appears on the USGS map (incorrectly). The map also shows a link trail up the Calhoun Basin to the Mansfield Ditch — which I've never found.

Description: From the trailhead, ride about half a mile to a fork in the trail at a metal stake. Up and right is the Hadley Gulch Trail, down and left is where you go. After half a mile the trail descends a short rock staircase—mind your ankles—and drops down to the creek. The foliage can get a bit jungle-like along here. Press on. The trail narrows even more and you will have a rock wall on your right, the creek on your left and a crumbling trail underfoot. A horse's natural claustrophobia can kick in here—that's why you need a seasoned horse — there isn't any room for disagreement! Drop down to the river bed, step over a log and up a steep rocky section (push, push, push!). On you go. The trail drops into the stream via a rock slab. Hopefully your horse will slither down it and not launch himself from the top as mine does. On your return, this slab will get wet from the horse in front of you—I have seen two horses lose their footing and slip sideways so be prepared. Wade upstream for 30 feet and jump back out on the right. Things calm down now but be very careful of two sections where the trail is narrow and eroding — keep your horse focussed on his feet and be prepared to bail.

The Main Elk trail will 'end' facing the crossing of Main Elk into Deep Creek. The trail is on the right hand side of the Deep Creek canyon, and a branch has been placed over the continuation of the Main Elk on your right. If you assume this is just a fallen branch and continue along Main Elk, you will end up in an old mining camp and will have to retrace your steps. Cross the creek. The trail is directly in front of you, but it can be hard to spot if the undergrowth is luxurious—I have built a cairn here. The trail now wanders back and forth across and along Deep Creek. Keep looking! It ends in a wide grassy basin at the remnants of an old cabin. Stop when you get tired of picking your way through fallen timber at a good lunch spot. Happy fishing!

Notes & Directions: Exit I70 N at New Castle, turn L or W into town. Take 7th Street N out of New Castle which becomes CR245. Turn R or N on CR243—Main Elk. Drive 6.3m to the end of Main Elk to the trailhead. Sections of trail are rocky.

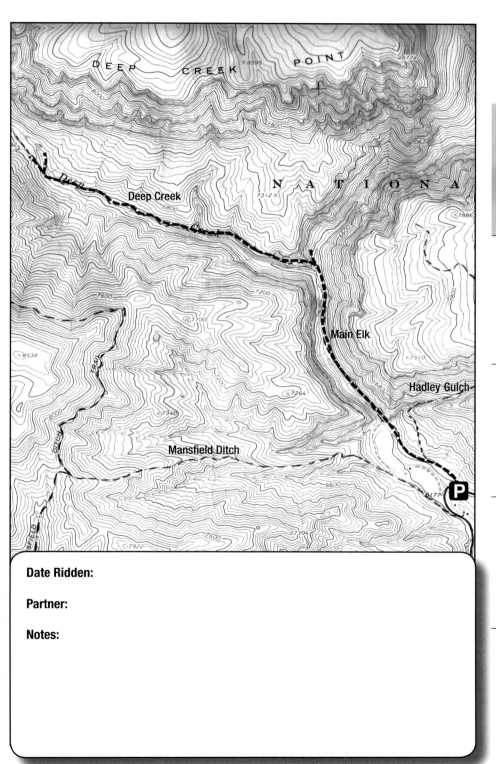

Date Ridden:

Partner:

Notes:

New Castle

Silt

Rifle

Rulison

Parachute

West Elk Ridge Loop

Grade: 2
Type: Loop
Time: 2 hours
USGS Quad: Rifle Falls

Description: Leave the BLM parking lot on the main trail. Immediately after crossing the ditch, turn R and follow the old West Elk Trail up to meet the main trail again. Turn right and drop down to a sage brush flat where the trail 'T' s. Turn right, following the trail left at the cattle pond as it turns north again. The trail rises and passes a cattle pond on the left, before taking a wide turn left and westwards. The trees disappear, replaced by oak brush. On your left, look for a grassy, sagey open area with an obvious cattle trail to a hard-to-see pond. The main trail turns sharp right and a grassy jeep trail will be dead ahead. Follow the jeep track to the 'edge' where it dead ends. At a large pine tree at 11O'clock, drop down a short rocky slope on a good elk trail. The elk trail turns rightwards, but continue downwards, weaving your way through open june berry brush and sage, looking for white tags. Join a jeep trail and turn left. The jeep trail hits a main trail, where you turn right back to the 'T'. Turn right at the 'T' and follow the jeep road back to the parking lot.

Notes & Directions: Exit I70 N to New Castle, turn L or W into town. Take 7th Street N out of New Castle which becomes CR245. Turn R at the National Forest Access sign 'Buford Road' CR245 about 4 miles out of town. Turn L on CR247 North Cutoff Road. The trailhead is 1.2m on the right. Best in spring and autumn.

A very pleasant loop with good views and cattle ponds along the way. The loop can be extended anywhere up on top by adding on some of the old prospect roads, one of which has a spectacular overlook into Rifle Creek drainage over a red cliff gorge.

Date Ridden:

Partner:

Notes:

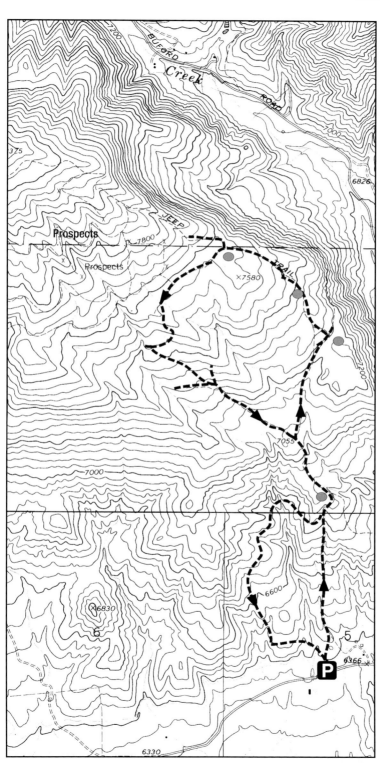

Cherry Stock Loop

Grade: 2
Type: Loop
Time: 3 to 3.5 hours
USGS Quad: Rifle Falls

Description: With your back to the reservoir, take the small uphill trail on your right from the parking lot. Go through, or around, a double gate, then a stock fence. Drop down to a post, where a large trail leads up and left (this is your return trail) and a smaller trail goes down and right. Go down and right, following a fenceline on your right down into the aspens along Cherry Creek. Cross the creek to meet up with the Cherry Creek Trail. Turn left. Follow the trail up and along the stream, eventually crossing it where it widens up into an open meadow with a stock fence running across you. The stream continues rightwards—you go left through a fence. At the next fenceline, turn left and go steeply uphill. The trail emerges from the aspens into a wide grassy area where the West Elk Stock Trail crosses in front of you. Turn left onto the West Elk Stock Trail. Drop down (there are a couple of short rocky sections to negotiate) to the post where you turn up and right back to the trailer.

Notes & Directions: Exit I70 N to New Castle, turn L or W into town. Take 7th Street N out of New Castle which becomes CR245. Turn right at the National Forest Access sign 'Buford Road' CR 245 about 4 miles out of town. Park 1.9 miles on from the cattle guard marking the National Forest Boundary directly opposite the reservoir.
   This is a loop connecting the Cherry Creek Trail with the West Elk Stock Trail. A good ride for hot days as it runs along a creek and is in the shade. It is gently up and down, and where the two trails meet, there are lots of flat loops that follow the ski trails that you can add on for more interest.

Date Ridden:

Partner:

Notes:

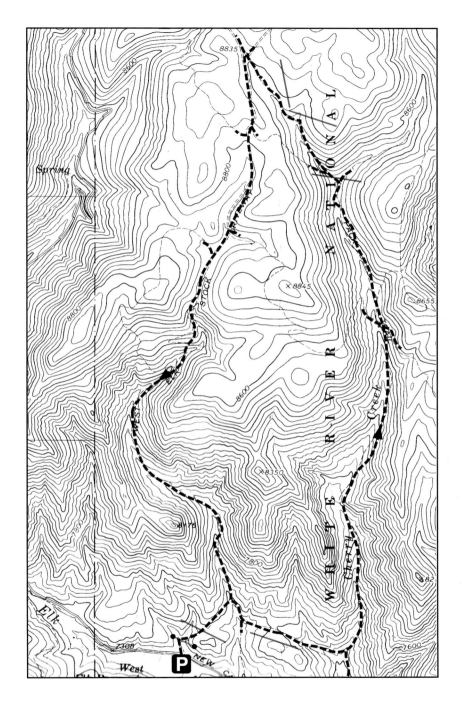

New Castle

Silt

Rifle

Rulison

Parachute

Baldy Creek

Grade: 2
Type: Out and Back
Time: 3.5 hours
USGS Quad: Center Mountain

Description: This is an excellent trail that wends its way up Baldy Creek to a hunting cabin where there is a spring-fed trough for the horses to drink from. From the gas well, continue riding up the road, following the State Lands signs. Go through the gate into the campsite and follow the trail that leads leftwards up Baldy Creek. The trail is wide, crossing the creek and a few little streams before taking a detour around a private cabin. Continue up to the hunting cabin, outhouse and corral.

You will see on the USGS Quad that a loop can be done that leaves the campsite on the right as you enter and returns back past the cabins. This loop takes about 5 hours to ride. I have not described the loop (lovely though it is) because it does require advanced trail finding skills in a couple of sections which are difficult to describe unless you have already tried the trail. Please remember there are no dogs allowed on GCSWA.

Notes & Directions: Exit I70 at New Castle. Turn S over the river, then west on CR335 to CR312. At CR312 turn S or L. At 6 miles turn R at the 'Y'. Drive up Baldy Creek for 5 miles and park and turn at a disused gas well. There is parking, turning and corrals further up at the trailhead/campground, but I strongly advise checking them out first as you ride past them! This is a good summer morning trail.

Garfield Creek State Wildlife Area is open to the public from July 15th to the 1st of December. It is comprised of two tracts of land: the Garfield Creek tract and the Baldy Creek tract. The Baldy tract is at a higher elevation and accesses Sunlight Mountain and the trails around there. The Garfield tract is lower and, by the time it is open to the public, the trails are too hot to ride. By the time it cools off, it is Hunting Season. Make no mistake, GCSWA positively seethes with hunters, so always check the seasons before riding there.

Date Ridden:

Partner:

Notes:

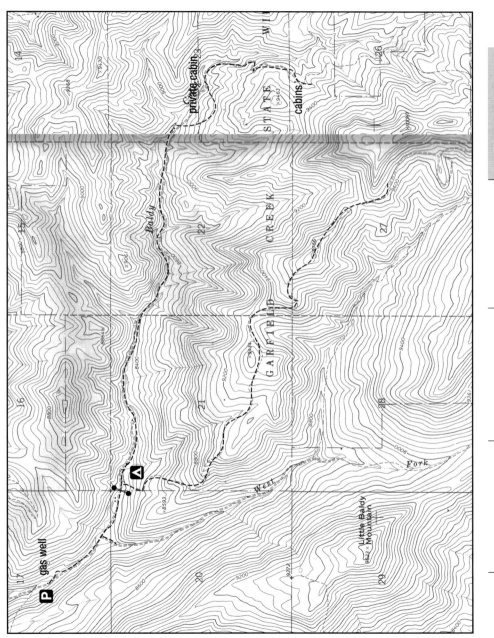

New Castle

Silt

Rifle

Rulison

Parachute

Center Mountain

Grade: 2
Type: Loop
Time: 4 to 5 hours
USGS Quad: Center Mountain

Description: This ride starts quite steeply but soon levels off. Follow the good trail up and leftwards. You will pass through a range gate and along and over a small stream. The trail turns left at an obvious T junction and drops down through aspen groves before crossing back through a range gate at a big cattle pond. The trail steepens in sections before hitting the ridge line at another range gate.

Through the gate is a cattle 'camp' with a large pond. Directly opposite you is a range gate. Do not go through it, but through the higher one to the right on an obvious trail. This trail follows the ridge line. Follow the ridge to where the trail splits and either goes down and left or up and right. Go down and left (the other trail follows the ridge and drops you steeply down to where you started). The trail drops gently down and along, paralleling Baldy Creek and passing through a couple of range gates. The trail continues to drop to Baldy Creek, and, at the closest point, you will decend a series of sharp switchbacks. At the third switchback—a N pointing one—you will see a trail leading north. If you have a dog or if it is before July 15th, you must take this trail which climbs for a bit before dropping you back down to the road about a quarter of a mile from the trailer. Stay left at the Y junctions.

If you do not have a dog and/or it is after July 15th, drop down to Baldy Creek through a green gate. Turn right and follow the road for about half a mile before crossing the creek at an obvious crossing on the right. Stay on the main trail (don't go right) and go through a range gate. At this point the creek will be on your left subsequently the ditch will be on your left. The trail crosses the ditch, but instead, go right and up a short stony trail to another meadow. Follow the jeep tracks in the center of the meadow down to the road. Turn right and it is about a mile to the trailer.

Notes & Directions: I70 to New Castle. Turn S over the river, then west on CR335 to CR312. At CR312 turn S or L. At mile 6 stay left at Y and the road turns to dirt. At 1.2 miles past the Y, park and turn on the left. Walk south for about 100 yds and opposite the house is the BLM gate on the right.

This trail starts steeply, but soon levels off. The return is also steep, so I prefer to follow Baldy Creek (and the horses can get a drink). However, because you are on Garfield Creek State Wildlife Area, you cannot have a dog, or ride before 15th July. Best ridden in early summer.

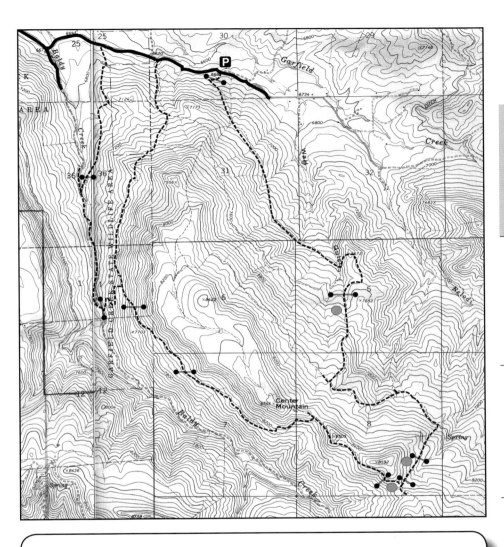

Date Ridden:

Partner:

Notes:

New Castle

Silt

Rifle

Rulison

Parachute

ROARING FORK VALLEY HORSE COUNCIL

Founded in 2004, our mission is to be a unified voice,
to preserve access to trails and support the future welfare
of horses and horsemanship.

Our goals are:
* TO CONTINUE TO DEVELOP AN ACTION-ORIENTED GROUP OF DEDICATED HORSE PEOPLE
* TO DEVELOP EDUCATIONAL PROGRAMS
* TO HOST TRAIL RIDES
* TO FURTHER INVOLVEMENT IN LOCAL AND REGIONAL EQUESTRIAN AND TRAIL ISSUES
* TO ORGANIZE SOCIAL ACTIVIES
* TO ESTABLISH AFFILIATION WITH THE COLORADO HORSE COUNCIL
* TO CREATE A HORSE WELFARE FUND TO PROVIDE CRITICAL CARE

All disciplines welcome!!

FOR MEMBERSHIP INFO AND TO LEARN MORE
www.roaringforkvalleyhorsecouncil.com

As the first horse organization of this kind
in Western Colorado, we welcome
your participation. 501C3 Non-Profit Status Pending.

Silt

	Grade
7. Harvey Gap Hogback	1
8. Harvey Gap Reservoir	2
9. Elk Flats	2
10. Burning Mountain Mine	1
11. Peach Valley	1
12. Gibson Gulch Loop	2
13. June Creek Loop	2

New Castle

Silt

Rifle

Rulison

Parachute

Harvey Gap Hogback

Grade: 1
Type: Out and back
Time: 2 hours
USGS Quad: Silt and New Castle

Description: A mostly level ride that runs along the lower slopes of the Hogback with views to the north and west on the way out and east across the reservoir on the way back. Just through the gate is a knoll, with a good view down to New Castle, this is a good place to stop for lunch or turn and go back. Once back in the parking lot, you can untack and lead your horse across the road for a drink in the reservoir.

Notes & Directions: from I70 Silt, exit N. Turn L or W along Main Street. Turn R or N on 1st to the intersection with Silt Mesa Road. Turn L or W for a mile or so. Turn R or N on Harvey Gap Road, signposted National Forest Access. Follow the road through L and R sharp bends up towards Harvey Gap Reservoir for 3.9 miles and the parking lot is on the right, through a gate.

Straight ahead of you is the Hogback trail as you enter the parking lot. I've not included a map as it is completely straight. There is a also a trail on the right out of the parking lot, and this is the steep trail up to the radio towers.

A good trail for hot summer mornings, beginners and leading children on ponies.

Date Ridden:

Partner:

Notes:

Harvey Gap Reservoir

Grade: 2
Type: Loops or shuttle
Time: 2 to 5 hours
USGS Quad: Silt

Description: This is a series of jeep tracks that wends through pinon forest above Harvey Gap Reservoir and along the Hogback west towards Rifle Gap with lovely views to the north. You can explore loops or even ride to Rifle Gap or Elk Flats (see pg. 30).

Notes & Directions: from I70 Silt, exit N. Turn L or W along Main Street. Turn R or N on 1st to the intersection with Silt Mesa Road. Turn L or W for a mile or so. Turn R or N on Harvey Gap Road, signposted National Forest Access. Follow the road through L and R sharp bends up towards Harvey Gap Reservoir. At 3.3 miles, just before and below the dam, is the parking lot. The trail is on the left as you enter the parking lot over the irrigation ditch, passing a burnt out bus (an object of deep suspicion).

Do not attempt to access this trail by riding up the west side of the dam unless you are confident that your horse can, and will, jump the concrete spillway!

Holds a little more snow than the 'front of the hogback' trails. Full summer sun, though picks up any breezes.

Date Ridden:

Partner:

Notes:

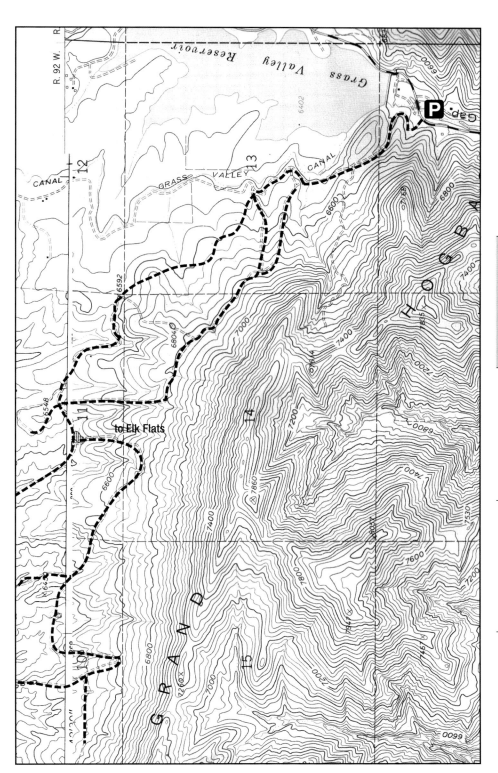

New Castle

Silt

Rifle

Rulison

Parachute

Elk Flats

Grade: 1
Type: Loops or Shuttle
Time: 1-5 hours
USGS Quad: Rifle Falls

Description: The trails wend their way through sage brush flats with some elevation gain and fine views to the north and east. There are a number of different loops (see map) you can do here and spend as much or as little time as you choose. A fine ride, either as a there and back (about 4 hours), or as a shuttle, is to ride to Harvey Gap Reservoir. As the name would suggest elk frequent the area making it a popular hunting spot.

Notes & Directions: from I70 Silt, exit N. Turn L or W along Main Street. Turn R or N on 1st to the intersection with Silt Mesa Road. Turn L or W for a mile or so. Turn R or N on Harvey Gap Road, signposted National Forest Access. Follow the road through L and R sharp bends up towards Harvey Gap Reservoir. Go past the reservoir to the intersection with CR226 Grass Valley. Turn L or W. Follow this road for 3.5 miles to a parking lot on the left.

Holds a little more snow than the 'front of the hogback' trails. Full summer sun, though picks up any breezes

If you want to extend your shuttle, a trail runs from Rifle Gap Reservoir to Harvey Gap Reservoir. To get to the trailhead, continue on CR226 to the intersection with SH325. Turn left. Go 0.2 miles past the entrance to the park. On the L is a small sign that says 'parking'. There is parking here, but it is too cramped to get a trailer in and out, so park on the opposite side of the road in the fee paying lot (and yes, you will have to pay!). The trail starts up the short, but steep little hill just behind the 'parking' sign, and meets up with the Elk Flats trail. It is considerably easier trail finding this way!

Date Ridden:

Partner:

Notes:

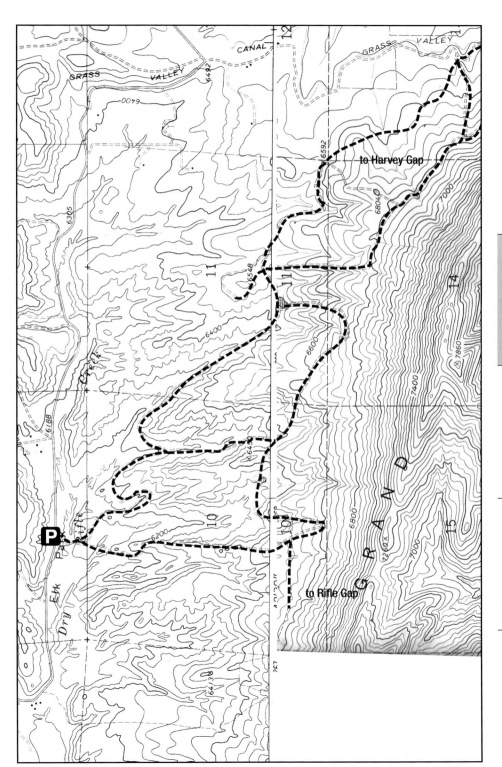

New Castle

Silt

Rifle

Rulison

Parachute

Burning Mountain Mine

Grade: 1
Type: Out and back
Time: 2 hours
USGS Quad: Silt and New Castle

Description: This trail winds through sage, cedar and pinon up into the Hogback, with good views down into Slaughter Gulch and across to Mamm Peak on the way back. The trail gets steadily narrower, until you are following a broad wash. Keep going and eventually you will reach obvious mine workings. There is a great flat grassy spot for a picnic about 250 yards before the trail peters out completely.

Notes & Directions: From I70 Silt, exit N. Turn R and follow US6/24 E. Turn L on CR235 to the intersection with Peach Valley Road. Turn L or W on Peach Valley Road. Follow this road as it bends R, northwards, and uphill. Just on the next bend, as the road is about to turn 90 degrees to the left (W) there is a pullout on the right. There is a dirt road here, framed by two tall posts, with a sign nailed to to the left one saying 'No Passing'. This is in fact CR298 and there is good trailer parking about a quarter of a mile up. Alternatively, start at the Peach Valley Ditch Trail parking lot (page 34).

Faces due south. Hot in summer and the wash fills with snow in winter, but excellent for those minimal-snow winter/early spring clear-blue-sky days.

This trail links with the Peach Valley trail (overleaf), making for a very pleasant outing. However— the first time you try the link, it is much easier to ride from the parking lot for the Peach Valley trail to the Burning Mountain trail because it is very easy to get lost in a series of promising, but incorrect trails, trying it the opposite way!

Date Ridden:

Partner:

Notes:

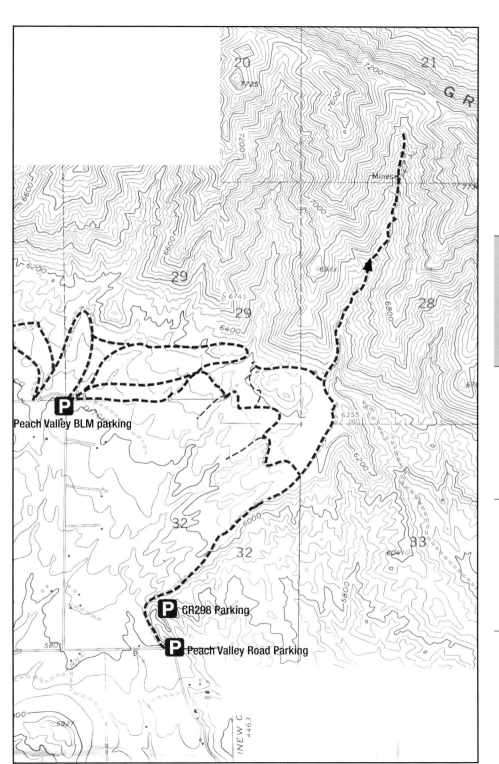

New Castle

Silt

Rifle

Rulison

Parachute

Peach Valley

Grade: 2
Type: Loops
Time: 2 hours
USGS Quad: Silt

Description: The area W of Burning Mountain Trail, almost to Harvey Gap is criss-crossed with trails made by people, horses, deer, elk, motorcycles and 4WD. The East Lateral ditch on the left is your southern boundary and a trail follows it, and fencelines, westwards, before petering out into game trails in the foothills. Along the way, lots of trails branch northwards running across lovely grassy mesas. This is a great area for low key trail riding and one of my favorite areas to condition horses in spring, as the trails are soft and gently undulating. I have not included a comprehensive map to the area, as part of the adventure is making your own loops.

Notes & Directions: From I70 Silt, exit N. Turn L and follow US6/24 west. Turn R on 4th Street to the intersection with Peach Valley Road. Turn R or E on Peach Valley Road. Turn L on CR250. Right on the 90 degree leftwards bend is a dirt road/parking lot/public lands access point on the right. There is ample parking here, but be aware that it is very uneven.
  The trail directly ahead of you as you pull in links to the Burning Mountain Mine Trail. There is evidence that the north end of the parking lot is used as a target range…

Date Ridden:

Partner:

Notes:

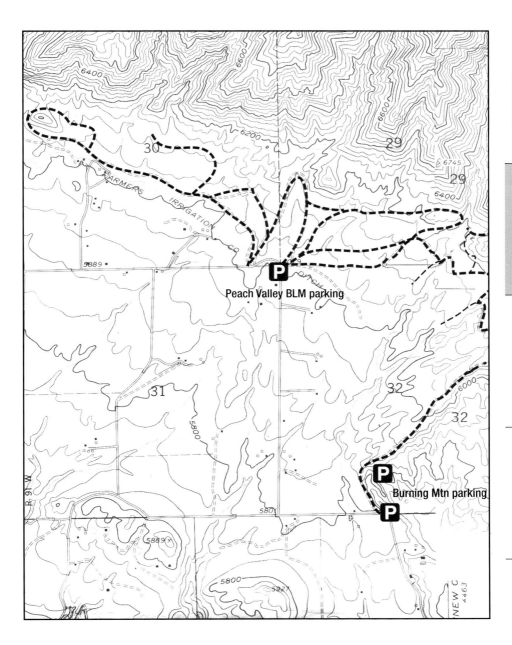

Peach Valley BLM parking

Burning Mtn parking

New Castle

Silt

Rifle

Rulison

Parachute

Gibson Gulch Loop

Grade: 2
Type: Loop
Time: 3 hours
USGS Quad: Gibson Gulch

Description: This is a very low key trail, with spectacular panoramic views. The elevation gain is very steady. There are a number of combinations of loops you can do, and of course, nothing says you have to stay on the road.... I have described just one. At the time of going to press, there was ample evidence that gas/oil wells were going to be drilled at some point. Once drilled, they won't detract from the experience, but I doubt meeting a drilling rig along the trail will enhance it much. I would check the drilling status with the Oil & Gas Commission or the BLM.

Ride up the road for about 45 minutes until you come to a large turning/parking area, a cattle pond and a 'T' junction. Turn right for a couple of hundred yards and look for a rough jeep trail that crosses the main trail. Take this trail left up to a cattle feeder. This trail will take you back east, passing above and behind the cattle pond you started from, crossing a jeep trail, to deposit you on a hairpin bend at another cattle feeder. Ride up the road, turning left at the fork to drop down into Gibson Gulch. Turn left at the bottom, by a large flat grassy area and follow the wash down, then back up, through a range fence and on up to a cattle pond. Turn right on the road and return back to the original pond.

Notes & Directions: Exit I70 S at Silt. Turn L or E along the frontage road, then turn R, or south, over the river. At the junction turn left (east) on CR346. Turn R or south on Divide Creek CR311. At 5.8 m is a pull out and dirt road over a cattle guard on your left. I choose to park here, just off the road or just over the cattleguard. There is parking further up, but I suggest you check it out first. There is also parking at the top of the road, but as the road is quite narrow with few pullouts, I can't risk it! This is a good spring ride. In autumn the aspens will be spectacular—on the other hand, there are an awful lot of berry bushes in Gibson Gulch ...

Date Ridden:

Partner:

Notes:

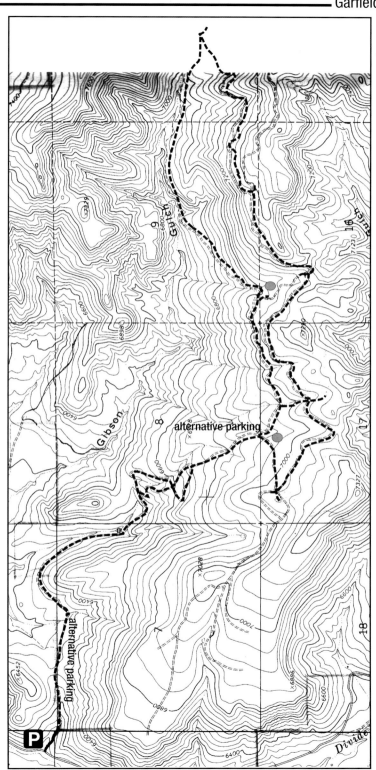

June Creek Loop

Grade: 2
Type: Loop
Time: 2-3 hours
USGS Quad: Gibson Gulch

Description: From the Uncle Bob parking lot, ride left and up FS road #8220 to a fork with a sign saying "June Creek Firewood Cutting." Turn left, or for a slightly longer loop, turn right. Drop down past a couple of ponds (the second pond is where you will come out, FS road#8252 through a range fence, if you do the long loop). Follow the road leftwards to a large grassy meadow. The road drops down and right (this is where you will come up from East Divide)—but continue across the meadow to pick up a good jeep trail that passes a stock tank. Take the right fork of the trail (level, not upwards) and continue on this more or less level trail with a few rocky sections to emerge back on the road you came up.

Notes & Directions: Exit I70 S at Silt. Turn L or E along the frontage road, then turn R, or south, over the river. At the junction turn left (east) on CR346. Turn R or south on Divide Creek CR311. This lovely loop with fabulous views can be accessed from either NFA East Divide or Uncle Bob. The East Divide access is 1.9m on the right up East Divide Creek Road. However, fording the creek will be the start of your ride. I strongly advise checking out both the parking and the depth of the creek before you commit! For the Uncle Bob access, continue on Divide Creek Road to just past mile marker 13 where you turn left over a cattle guard. Continue up over a couple of cattle guards, until you come to a large parking and turning area about 1.7m further on, with a sign that says 'Certified Weed Free Hay Area'. This is a good ride for warm days and there are a lot of lovely trails to do around here.

Date Ridden:

Partner:

Notes:

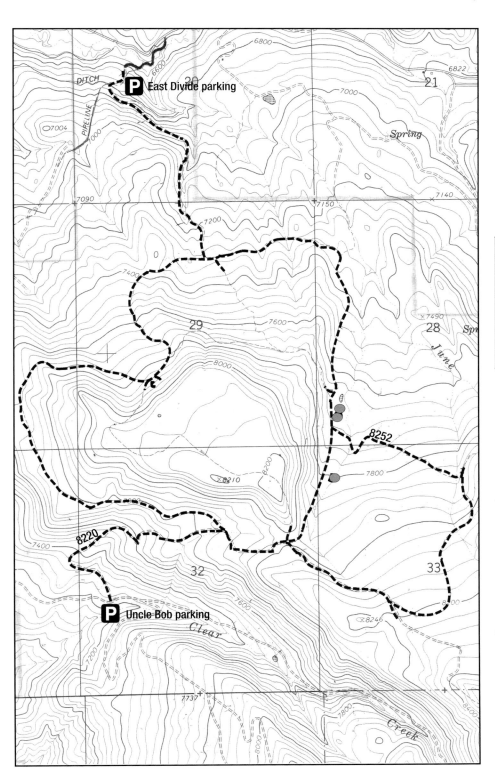

C2K RANCH
HORSE BOARDING · HORSESHOEING · HORSE HAULING

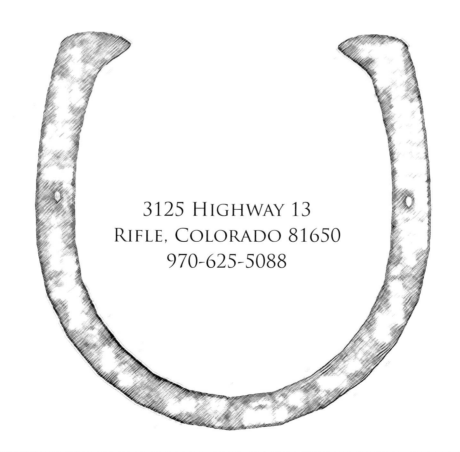

3125 HIGHWAY 13
RIFLE, COLORADO 81650
970-625-5088

Rifle

New Castle

Silt

Rifle

Rulison

Parachute

Tipple Mine

Grade: 1
Type: Out and back
Time: 2 hours
USGS Quad: Silt

Description: This is one of my favorites. The trail follows the old mine road. Rising steadily through increasingly dramatic scenery, passing through a rock 'gate,' and up the hogback, it ends in a dramatic overview on the north side of the hogback, looking across Rifle Gap Reservoir and the Flattops.

Notes & Directions: From I70 exit N to Rifle. Take Railroad Avenue N and continue on US13 towards Craig and Meeker. Approx. 2 miles out of town, turn R on SH325 towards Rifle Gap Reservoir. At 1.5 miles, turn R on CR251(N Hasse). Follow this as it turns to dirt, past some houses and up a steepish little rise. Go past the red roofed barn and the parking lot is 500 or so yards further on at the end of the wire fence on the left. There is another parking lot further on if this one is wallowing in mud.

Faces due south. Hot in summer but good in low snow winters, with only the very top being really snowy.

Date Ridden:

Partner:

Notes:

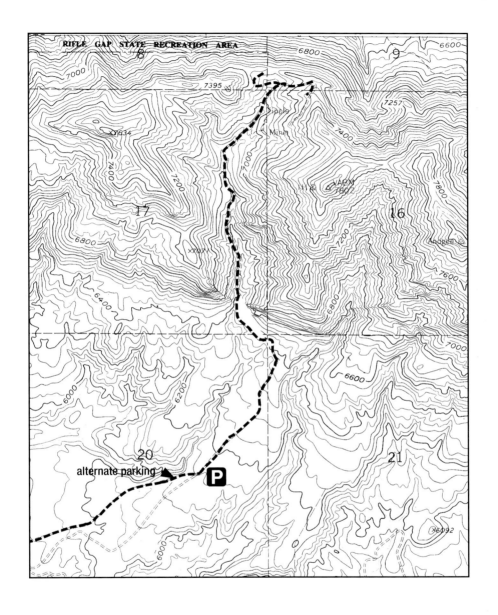

New Castle

Silt

Rifle

Rulison

Parachute

Estes Gulch Mine

Grade: 1
Type: Out and back
Time: 2 to 2.5 hours
USGS Quad: Rifle

Description: Very similar to the Burning Mountain ride, but more open and with impressive mining remains. Leave the pullout and walk down the road towards Rifle (south) for 200 yards. Just at a 35mph/RH bend sign is a dirt road/trail on the right. Follow the obvious trail as it skirts above the golf course, staying right at the fork. There are a few side trails up here, but the main one is obvious. The wide trail peters out in a wash, but keep going until you get to the very large mine remains. Stay right at the willow patch.

Notes & Directions: From I70 exit R or N to Rifle. Take Railroad Avenue N and continue on US13 towards Craig and Meeker. Approx. 2 miles out of town, turn R on SH325 towards Rifle Gap Reservoir. At mile marker 2 is a dirt road on the left which is the start of the trail. There is a good pullout/turnaround on the left 0.1 miles further on. Coming from Rifle Gap, the pullout is on the right, past the golf course and just at a LH bend/35mph sign.

Faces due south. Good winter ride, too hot for summer (and too leafy in the willow patch!).

The trail can also be started from SH13, which has the advantage of no road riding if you have dogs with you. The trail head is on the right, 2.4 miles past the SH325 turn. Park on the right as you pull in and ride up the road before dropping down right just before the gate. Follow the pylons and head left at the fork (the first left at the pond will loop you around a nice sage brush mesa) to join the main trail at the next fork.

Date Ridden:

Partner:

Notes:

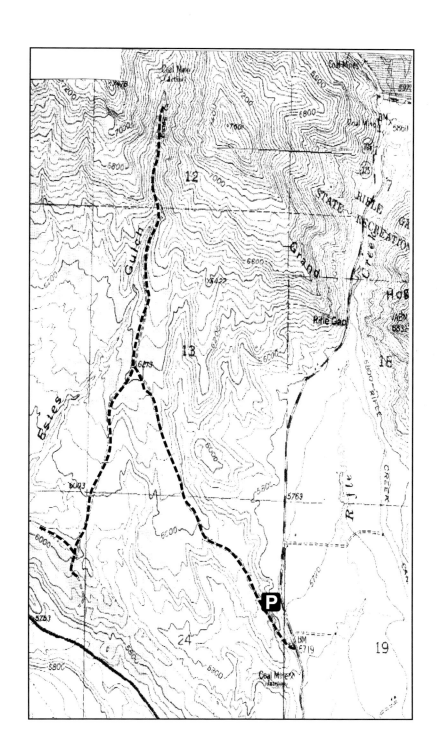

New Castle

Silt

Rifle

Rulison

Parachute

West Rifle Creek SWA

Grade: 1
Type: Loops
Time: 1-2 hours
USGS Quad: Horse Mountain

Description: This loop has some road riding, but it is a very pleasant outing. The trail arrives back at the road at a parking lot 0.4 miles on the left before the Y where you are parked. You could also start the trail here—the parking lot is big enough for trailers. However this lot is also a shooting range and whilst I have never heard shots during the week, I have on weekends.

From the intersection parking, ride N along CR252 for approximately half a mile. Go through the third wire gate on the left (the first pair count as one), down and across the stream. Go R at the first trail fork, turning L at the next obvious trail which takes you back along towards the reservoir (if you continued upwards, you will get to the old mine, in itself a nice trail with an overlook at the end). Follow the trail, turning right at the gully crossing. Towards the end of the trail, you will head down a steep hill. which turns a bend into the shooting lot. If you hear shooting, turn leftwards and go through a wire gate, across the field, to exit onto the road through another gate just before the bridge. Otherwise, continue to the parking lot, exit to the road and turn left. Ride back to the intersection.

Notes & Directions: From I70 exit N to Rifle. Take Railroad Avenue N and continue on US13 towards Craig and Meeker. Approx. 2 miles out of town, turn R on SH325 to Rifle Gap Reservoir. Turn L at the reservoir and follow CR252 W Rifle Creek for 2.1 miles to the Y intersection of CR252 and CR219. I suggest you park here. The first parking lot is at 1.7m, the intersection is at 2.1 miles and the third parking lot is 0.5m along the left hand fork of the intersection.

Holds a little more snow than the 'front of the hogback' trails. Full summer sun, though picks up any breezes.

Date Ridden:

Partner:

Notes:

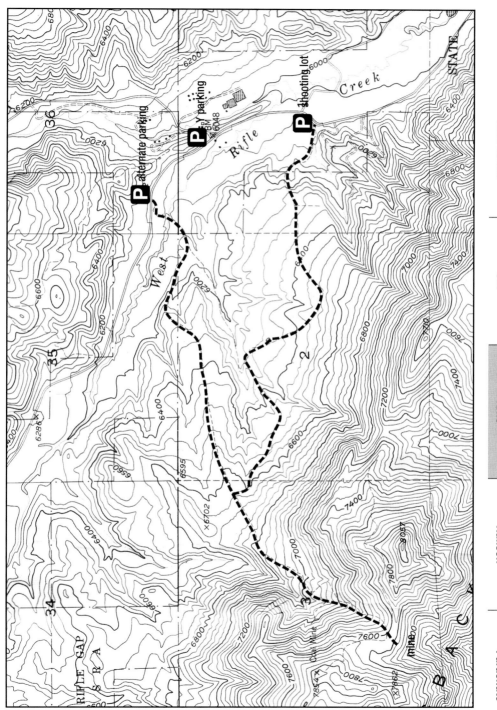

West Rifle Creek Loop

Grade: 3
Type: Loop
Time: 4 hours
USGS Quad: Horse Mountain

Description: This trail starts quite steeply but soon mellows. It wends its way through pinon forest up to open sage and oakbrush flats with excellent views all round. There are often cattle on top. Descend onto the road 1.3m further on from where you parked. There is a network of trails up on top leading you to Horse Mountain.

Notes & Directions: From I70 exit N to Rifle. Take Railroad Avenue N and continue on US13 towards Craig and Meeker. Approx. 2 miles out of town, turn R on SH325 to Rifle Gap Reservoir. Turn L at the reservoir and follow CR252 W Rifle Creek for 2.1 miles to the Y intersection of CR252 and CR219. Take the left fork CR252 for 3.6 miles to a dirt pullout on the right.

Faces south and is high enough to retain the snow. Late spring, early summer, fall and early low snow winters. Hot in summer. Some sections are rocky.

Date Ridden:

Partner:

Notes:

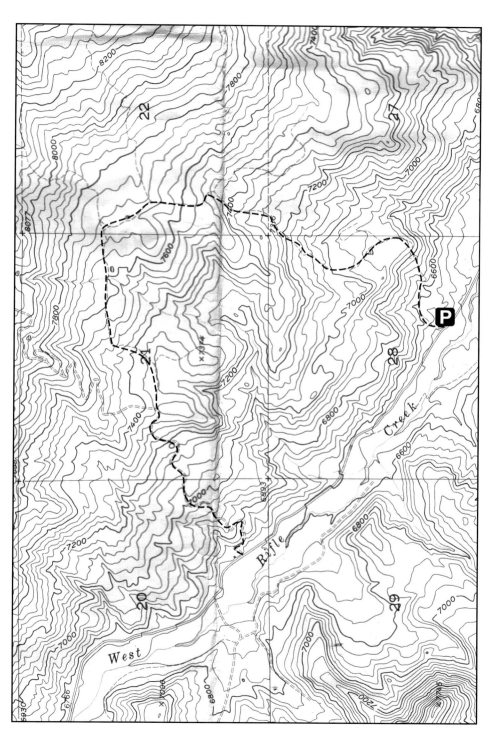

New Castle

Silt

Rifle

Rulison

Parachute

Butler Cabin

Grade: 3
Type: Out and back
Time: 3 to 4 hours
USGS Quad: Horse Mountain

Description: This is a pretty steep up and downish sort of trail, but I include it because it is the only way into Butler Creek. Follow the trail out of the parking lot, bearing left at the fork, to the end parking loop. The trail continues steeply down through a spruce and fir forest to a sage brush flat. This section is quite rocky. Go through the gate and turn right (paralleling the Puma Paw Ranch fence) and follow the trail across fallen cottonwoods into Butler Creek, where there is an old cabin and farm equipment.

Notes & Directions: From I70 exit N to Rifle. Take Railroad Avenue N and continue on US13 towards Craig and Meeker. Approximately 2 miles out of town, turn R on SH325 to Rifle Gap Reservoir. Turn L at the reservoir and follow CR252 W Rifle Creek to the Y intersection of CR252 and CR219. Bear right at the Y and continue past the prison for about half a mile until you see some corrals on your right and all sorts of parking options. The trail is obvious on the right at the second parking 'lot'.

Good late spring ride. Pretty steep, so make sure your horse is fit. You could also shuttle this trail back to the Sage Campground at Rifle Gap Reservoir if you go right at the first fork, which will bring you to the big cattle pond mentioned in the Ward Gulch Loop ride (page 53).

Date Ridden:

Partner:

Notes:

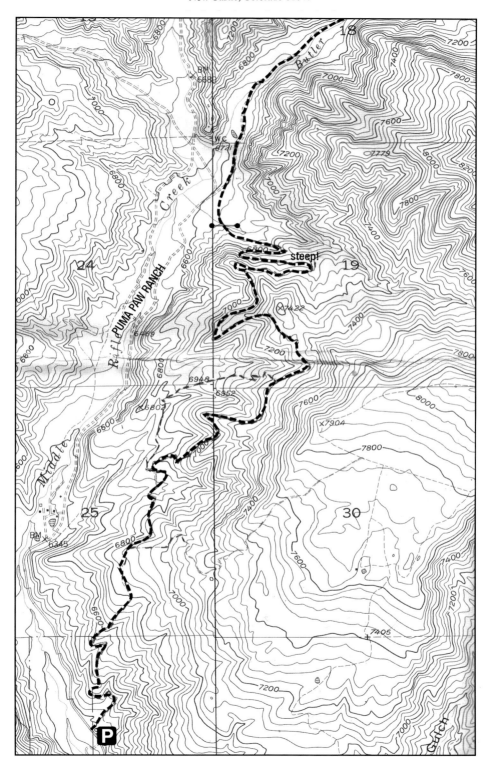

Rifle Gap Reservoir

These trails leave from the Sage Campsite. There is no fee if you park beyond the 'gate' at the north end of the campground, just let the Park staff know what you are doing.

Directions: From I70 exit N to Rifle. Take Railroad Avenue N and continue on US13 towards Craig and Meeker. Approx. 2 miles out of town, turn R on SH325 to Rifle Gap Reservoir. Turn R at the reservoir and continue round to the park entrance on the east side. Stop at the entrance fee booth. Follow the park road and Sage Campground is on your right. Follow the campground loop to the northernmost point, drive through the 'gate' in the fence, and park.

Ward Gulch

Grade: 1
Type: Out and back
Time: 2 hours
USGS Quad: Rifle Falls

Description: This trail (see map page 55) is added for completeness more than anything—but it is a pleasant short outing. Head up the trail and turn immediately left after the cattle guard. After 100 yards or so turn left again and head down into Ward Gulch. Turn right at the 'T' junction. The trail follows Ward Gulch, crossing a fairly wide draw on the way just after a quite rocky section, eventually ending up in a series of blind dead ends—I tried to follow it all the way but got stymied by dead trees so I don't know if it eventually ends up on top or not!

This is a good trail for spring, but wait for some drying time as I think it could be horribly squelchy right after a thaw.

Date Ridden:

Partner:

Notes:

Ward Loop

Grade: 2
Type: Loop
Time: 4 hours

Description: A long loop around Ward Gulch (see map page 55). Whilst this is a low key trail, following a jeep trail, it is steep and long, so your horse should be fit before you attempt it. From the Sage Campground, head north on the main trail. Follow the trail (marked with a brown Forest Service Road 8009 sign) ignoring all side shoots. The trail runs along the crest of the ridge at the top of Ward Gulch with wonderful views all round. Once past the gulch, stay on the trail, but look out for a big cattle pond in the sagebrush below and to your left. Ride to the pond and pick up the main trail leading south and down from the pond. The return is not as steep as the ascent, but is is quite rocky in places and there is one short, very steep section. The trail drops down through a range fence at the bottom of the last hill. You will ride past a cattle pond and through the fence again. Almost immediately turn left through another range fence to head back up Ward Gulch. At the first Y stay right and cross a gully. Stay right at the second Y and cross the gulch, before heading back uphill to join the main trail shortly uphill from the cattleguard you crossed on the way out. Turn right and head back down to the trailer.

New Castle

Silt

Rifle

Rulison

Parachute

Date Ridden:

Partner:

Notes:

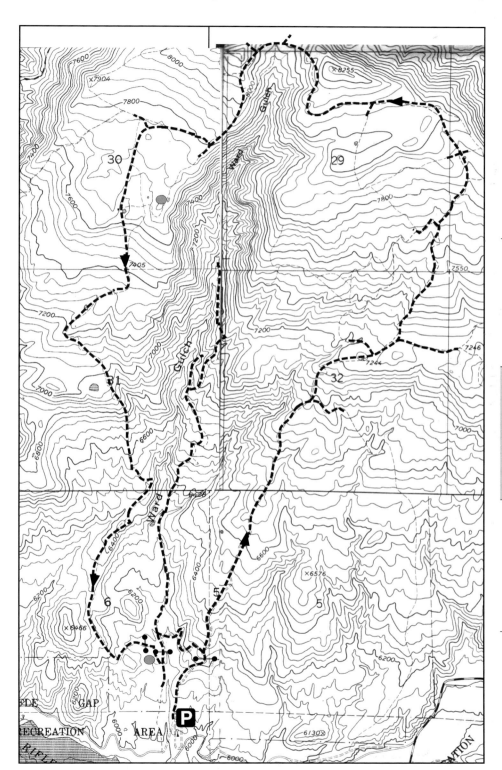

New Castle

Silt

Rifle

Rulison

Parachute

Helmer Gulch

Grade: 2
Type: Loop
Time: 2.5 to 3 hours
USGS Quad: Rifle

Description: This is a very pleasant outing, although a little steep to start and finish. Ride along the gravel road south, turning right just before the cattleguard and following the trail leftwards and up to a range fence and gate (the gate opens on the left). The trail follows a short but steep ridge to a line of pylons. Follow the pylons west (R). After a few miles, you will crest a hill with a big view of the distant mountains to the southwest. In the near distance, some houses will appear. Turn left (or south) just before an orange metal stake following a narrow rocky trail that will lead you along a short ridge before dropping you down to the pipeline. Turn left (east) and follow the pipeline for about 50 yds. The 'prospect road HG' will appear on your left. Follow this trail, which more or less follows the pipeline. The trail crosses the pipeline a few times. The last crossing will be from north to south and you will find yourself at a cattle pond and will see a private property fence on your right. Follow the cattle trail past the pond and back over the pipeline. The terrain changes to a moonscape of boulders, grass and dead trees. Follow the obvious cattle trail east. You will travel through the moonscape into a pinon juniper forest to emerge onto a grassy mesa with an obvious cattle pond and pylons running north/south. Head for the leftmost pylon and turn left, or north, down the obvious trail back to the trailer. Should you fail to find the cattle trails, follow the pipeline until you hit the line of pylons and turn north, left and/or down hill!

Notes & Directions: Exit I70 South at Rifle to the traffic lights. Turn right, following the road around a left 90 degree bend to a T junction. Turn R on CR320. At 1.3 miles, turn left onto a gravel road where you can park and turn. There is also parking/turning just before the gravel road, on the right, just past the Seventh Day Adventist Church.

Date Ridden:

Partner:

Notes:

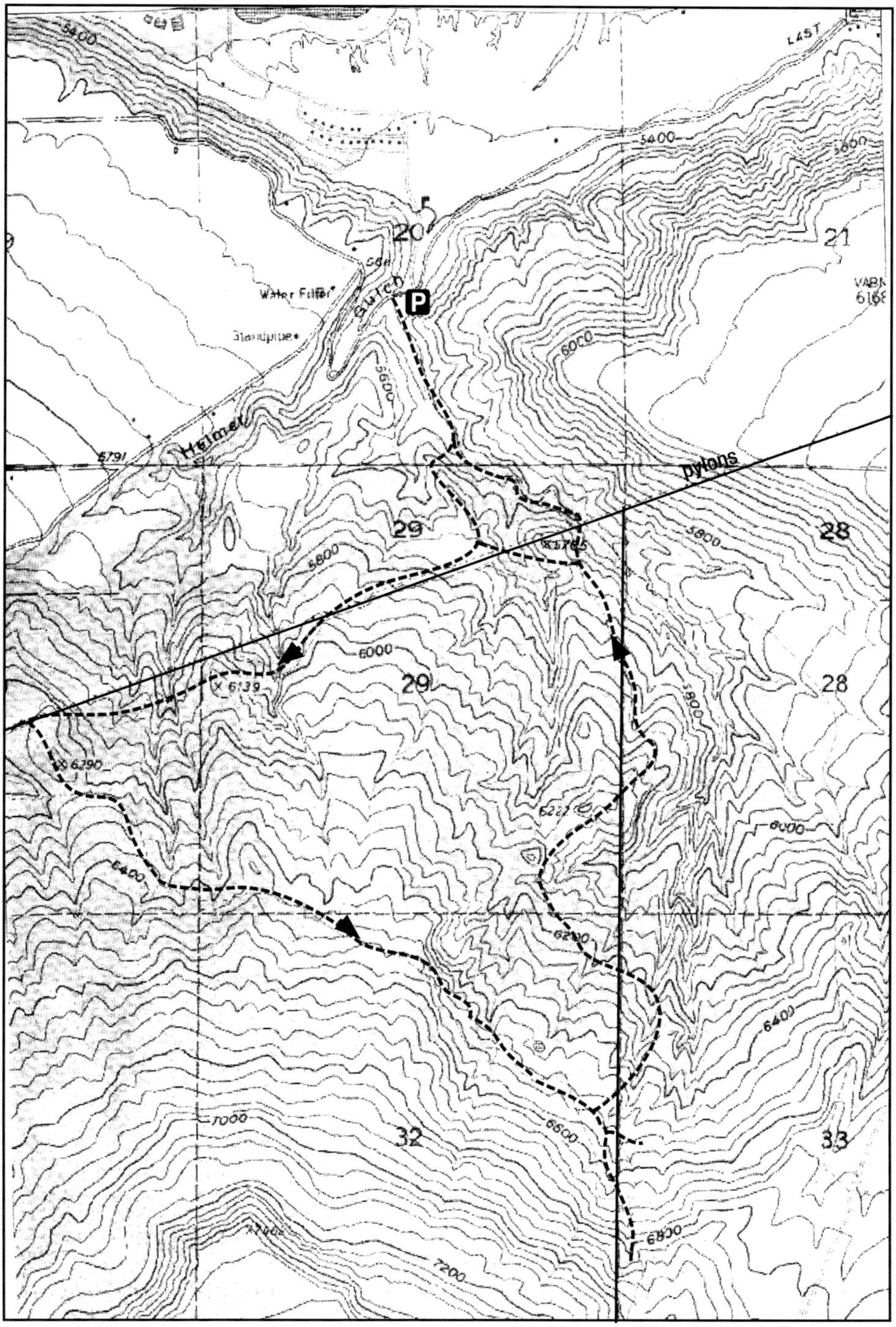
5400
LAST
5400
5800
20
21
Water Filter
Gulch
P
Standpipe
5600
6000
VABM
Helmet
5791
pylons
29
28
5800
5800
X 5765
X 6139
6000
29
28
5800
6290
6222
6000
6400
6200
6400
7000
32
6600
33
6800
7400
7200

Photo: Dave Pegg.

Parachute

Grade

New Castle

Silt

Rifle

Rulison

Parachute

Mount Logan

I am indebted to Bill and Diana Erickson for sharing this beautiful area with me.

This area stretches from Parachute to Roan Creek. The first access is in Garfield County and the second in Mesa County—but only just. It is a huge area of sage brush flats, pinon and juniper stands and rock walled canyons. Cattle are grazed up here, the dates are posted on the gates and there are range fences and cattle ponds all over. There are no limits (except your imagination) to where and for how long you can ride. I suggest that you ride The Pipeline first to get a general feel for the country and then the Long Loop. Overleaf I have drawn a map (not really accurate, but the best I can do!) that shows you the major reference points that you will find yourself returning to often. The descriptions sound complex, but they should make sense—at any rate, with Mt Logan to the north and I70 to the south, you can never get really lost, just delayed! Plan on spending 3 or so hours to ride each trail that I've described.

The Pipeline

Grade: 1
Time: 3 hours

Description: From the parking area ride north for 50 yards to the pipeline on an obvious jeep track. Turn west (or left) and follow the pipeline. After quarter of a mile or so, you will drop down a steep gully with a large boulder on the slope. Look left and you will see a huge boulder in the draw. Remember this! After half a mile or so further along the pipeline you will encounter a rock filled slope and a range fence that will force you to turn N or R, slightly back on yourself. Pick up a cow trail that will drop you down across the draw and onto a jeep trail. Head left or south to the range fence and the pipeline. Go through the wire gate (A) and cross the pipeline. Do not follow the jeep trail south, but head west up a grassy slope onto a sage brush mesa. Turn slightly NW to cross the range fence on a big jeep trail. Follow the trail to the pipeline and stay on the pipeline as the jeep trail heads left. About half a mile on, go left or south on a distinctive jeep trail down to the crossroads pond (the pipeline goes down a major gully just after this, so you don't really have much choice). This pond is a major landmark. Turn left on the trail (east and south). This big jeep trail forks at the top of the hill. The right hand fork will take you across a sage brush mesa to good views and fine lunch spots. After lunch retrace your steps back to the fork. Go right, or east, for a couple of hundred yards to the pipeline. Cross the pipeline to the cattlepond. Pick up a cattle trail heading north to another pond, follow the trail over a salt stained wash to the range fence gate (B). Again follow the cattle trails rightwards to two more ponds. Cross the jeep trail (this is the same one you turned left on to go through gate A and the draw and head back up the hill. Remember the boulder? Cross the draw here and head back to the trailer.

Date Ridden:

Partner:

Notes:

Notes & Directions: Exit I70 north at Parachute. Turn left (west) along US6/24. Continue through Parachute and onward to where the road crosses over I70. Turn R 6m past the end of the guard rails of the overpass. Drive under the overpasses over the cattle guard. Drive up the tarmac road which turns to dirt. Just through the old wire fence is a turning and parking area.

For the long loop, drive 2.6 miles further west along US6/24, crossing back over I70 and turn R or N. On your left is a red barn and on your right is an impressive collection of tires. About 100 yards past the barn, pull in through the BLM gate on the right into a good big parking area.

The Long Loop

Grade: 1
Time: 3 hours

Description: Head up the short but steep dirt trail on the NW of the parking lot (more or less opposite you as you pull in). The trail crests the top of the canyon and forks. Take the right hand fork and drop down onto a sage brush mesa. Follow the trail north to two large ponds. From the first pond head eastwards, paralleling an east/west range fence, towards a north/south orange staked range fence on good cow trails. Follow the trail through a range gate at the junction of the two fences. Go left along the fenceline which does a 90 degree turn to the right. Keep following it through a 'portal'. Follow the jeep trail east and south, crossing two 'creeks' to the crossroads pond. Four trails converge here, and you want to go right, south/south-west downwards and back to the trailer. If you find yourself heading up and north or up and south-east—you picked the wrong one!

Notes: The second, fenced, pond on the long loop has good jeep trails to explore all the way to Roan Creek. By the time you have done both of these trails, you will have a pretty good idea of the lay of the land and now you can wander at will. Remember the boulder descibed in the Pipeline ride? That's the only place you can cross this draw.

Mount Logan Map

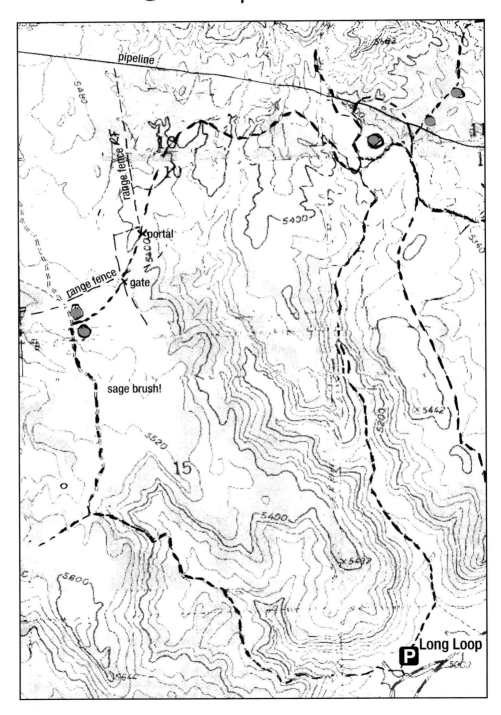

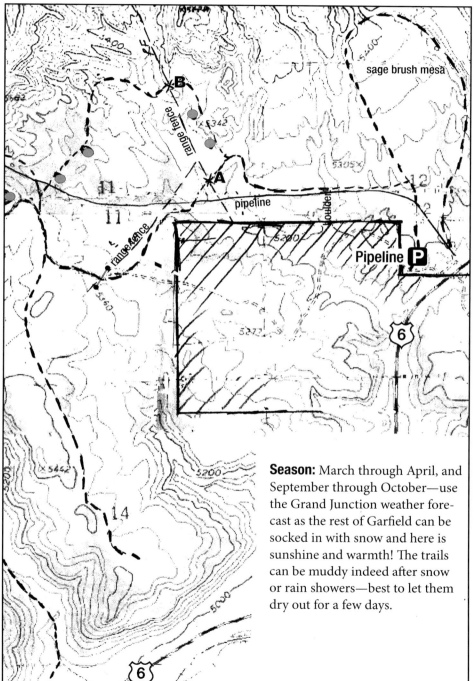

New Castle

Silt

Rifle

Rulison

Parachute

Season: March through April, and September through October—use the Grand Junction weather forecast as the rest of Garfield can be socked in with snow and here is sunshine and warmth! The trails can be muddy indeed after snow or rain showers—best to let them dry out for a few days.

About the Author

Fiona Lloyd is a landscape architect. She lives in New Castle, Colorado, with her husband, two cats, two dogs and three horses. Originally from England, she moved to Colorado in 1994, attracted by the prospect of being able to ride under endless blue skies.

Acknowledgments

My husband, without whom nothing is possible. My mother, without whom nothing would have been possible. A great number of people helped me with this book: the BLM and DOW staff, Chuck Shupe, Annette Wescott, Ned and Penny Dobson, Claira and Lily Thorsen, Bill and Diana Erickson and Diana Vagneur. Last but not least, Storm, Fancy and Hattie; my horses, my teachers.